NATURE UNDERCOVER

Published in the United States in 2000
by Blackbirch Press, Inc.
260 Amity Road
Woodbridge, CT 06525
web site: http://www.blackbirch.com
e-mail: staff@blackbirch.com

Courtship was created and produced by
McRae Books Srl, via de' Rustici, 5 – Florence (Italy)
e-mail: mcrae@tin.it

Text: Beatrice McLeod
Illustrations: Antonella Pastorelli, Paola Holguin, Andrea Ricciardi di Gaudesi, Ivan Stalio, Matteo Chesi
Picture research: Anne McRae
Graphic Design: Marco Nardi
Layout and cutouts: Adriano Nardi and Ornella Fassio
Color separations Litocolor, Florence

Printed in China

10 9 8 7 6 5 4 3 2 1

Library of Congress Cataloging-in-Publication Data
McLeod, Beatrice.
    Courtship / by Beatrice McLeod.
    p. cm.
    Includes index.
    ISBN 1-56711-503-9 (hardcover)
    1. Courtship of animals—Juvenile literature. [1. Animals—Courtship. 2. Animals—Habits and behavior.] I. Title
QL761.M385 2000
591.56'2—cd21
                        00–009749

NATURE UNDERCOVER

Courtship

Beatrice McLeod

Illustrations by Antonella Pastorelli, Paola Holguín, Ivan Stalio

Series Consultant:
Jim Kenagy, Professor of Zoology and Curator of Mammals,
Burke Museum of Natural History and Culture, University of Washington

BLACKBIRCH PRESS, INC.

WOODBRIDGE, CONNECTICUT

Contents

Snails, page 36

Siamese fighting fish, page 27

Introduction 7

Courtship *8-11*

Displays and Visual Cues *12-15*

Choosing a Partner *16-19*

Bighorn sheep, page 19

Offerings *20-23*

Hares, page 18

Fighting It Out *24-27*

Nests and Dens *28-31*

Dangers *32-35*

Mating *36-37*

For More Information 38

Index 38

Elephant seals, page 26

Atlas beetle, page 15

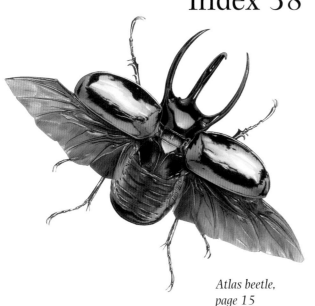

Introduction

Courtship and mating are critical steps in the life cycles of most animals. The drive to reproduce is a strong instinct. Courtship behaviors often begin with males fighting to establish breeding territories or dominance over females. A male may also perform elaborate dances or displays, prepare nests or dens, or offer gifts as an enticement to allow him to mate with a female. When courtship is successful, mating follows. When mating is successful, a new generation of animals is produced—a generation that will eventually take their parents' place in the animal kingdom.

Blue-footed boobie, page 14

How this book works

Courtship
"WATER DANCE." During courtship, male and female humpback whales "dance" together. The dance includes leaping out of the water, arching onto their backs with their flippers raised, and then sinking gracefully back into the waves. Despite their enormous size (a full-grown male can weigh more than 35 tons!), the ritual is an elegant, carefully executed display of power, grace, and energy.

Each chapter in this book begins with a stunning, two-page illustration that shows animals courting, reproducing, and surviving in their natural habitats. These openers lead into double-page spreads that show a variety of animals caught up in the cycle of life—driven, in part, by their instinct to reproduce and make more of their kind.

Brief captions explain how each spot illustration relates to the subject.

Vivid, descriptive text accompanies a large illustration that provides a stunning, up-close view of nature in action.

The introductory text gives an overview of the subject.

A dynamic, full-color illustration introduces each section subject.

Detailed illustrations highlight specific adaptations.

Courtship

As the mating season approaches, animals use a wide variety of techniques to attract partners. Some use elaborate displays of feathers or color, while others have vocal signals, such as roaring or singing to attract attention. Still others, including the male sable antelope, use physical contact—such as kicking— to attract a partner. Sometimes animals of the same sex use displays to discourage one another from competing for the same mates. When a mate is finally found, an elaborate series of other courtship rituals often follow.

Courtship

"WATER DANCE." During courtship, male and female humpback whales "dance" together. The dance includes leaping out of the water, arching onto their backs with their flippers raised, and then sinking gracefully back into the waves. Despite their enormous size (a full-grown male can weigh more than 35 tons!), the ritual is an elegant, carefully executed display of power, grace, and energy.

Courtship

As the mating season approaches, animals use a wide variety of techniques to attract partners. Some use elaborate displays of feathers or color, while others have vocal signals, such as roaring or singing to attract attention. Still others, including the male sable antelope, use physical contact—such as kicking—to attract a partner. Sometimes animals of the same sex use displays to discourage one another from competing for the same mates. When a mate is finally found, an elaborate series of other courtship rituals often follow.

In spring, a male **great reed warbler** marks out a territory that includes a quiet place for a female bird to lay her eggs. Then he sits on a tall reed and begins to sing a shrill courting song to attract a partner.

During courtship, male **hoverflies** search for mates where they are most likely to feed. When a male locates a female, he hovers above her, emitting a high-pitched whine, for about 10 minutes before diving down to mate.

Pikas are small mammals that are related to hares and rabbits. They live in North America, Asia, and western Europe. Pikas are territorial animals, with each individual occupying a small area. During the breeding season, the males emit a series of long calls to attract females. When a neighboring female replies, the two form a pair and stay together.

Many birds use displays to attract partners. **Whooper swans** conduct a mutual display before mating. This usually involves standing face to face with their wings outstretched while dipping their bills up and down at the same time. If the display is successful, the birds bond for life. Both the males, called cobs, and the females, called pens, help bring up the young babies, called cygnets.

In the fall, male **elk,** called stags, hold roaring contests to compete for the rights to groups of up to 20 females. The males emits about five very loud bellows per minute. The call is used to establish dominance over other males. The loudest animal wins and is recognized by the others as the most dominant.

During their brief mating season, male **frogs** use a series of loud croaking calls to attract females. To make their calls louder, many species have an inflatable vocal sac on their throats.

Humpbacks are among the most vocal species of whales. They string together a variety of calls—which sound like moans, cries, groans, and snores—into repeatable "songs" that can last for up to 35 minutes. Biologists are not sure of the exact purpose of the songs, but many believe the vocalizations help males and females communicate during courtship.

Among antelopes during courtship, the males often raise one foreleg to point at, or kick, the female. This gesture tells the female that the male is interested in mating. This **sable antelope** is kicking a female.

Marmots hibernate during the winter. When spring comes, males and females engage in courtship rituals that involve physical contact.

Displays and Visual Cues

FANTASTIC FEATHERS! To attract a female's attention during courtship, a male peacock spreads the 200-or-more stunning, iridescent feathers in his tail. Each feather is adorned with a bright "eye." He then performs a stately dance, showing her his magnificent tail first from behind and then from other angles. If the female is attracted, she will mate with him.

Mandrills live in the rain forests of central Africa. The average adult male can weigh up to 45 pounds (20 kg) and can be almost twice as large as the female. Males have bright red-and-blue coloring on their faces, which becomes even brighter during courtship to attract females.

Blue-footed boobies breed on the west coast of tropical South America. They share their breeding grounds with red-footed boobies, which—except for foot color—are nearly identical. To attract blue-footed boobie females—and to distinguish themselves from their red-footed neighbors—the male blue-footed boobies perform a special dance and raise their bright blue feet in the air one by one.

Displays and Visual Cues

In some animal species, the males and females are quite different in size and coloring. Often, the male animal is larger, more brightly colored, and more aggressive than the female—although sometimes it is the other way around. These differences help animals to recognize and choose the best partners during courtship. Many animals, particularly birds, perform special courtship displays to make themselves even more attractive to the opposite sex. Displays can include dancing, dramatic movements, and flashing or spreading brightly colored body parts or feathers.

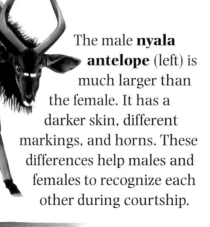

The male **nyala antelope** (left) is much larger than the female. It has a darker skin, different markings, and horns. These differences help males and females to recognize each other during courtship.

The male **great argus pheasant** has very long feathers on its tail and wings, which it fans out into a marvelous display during courtship.

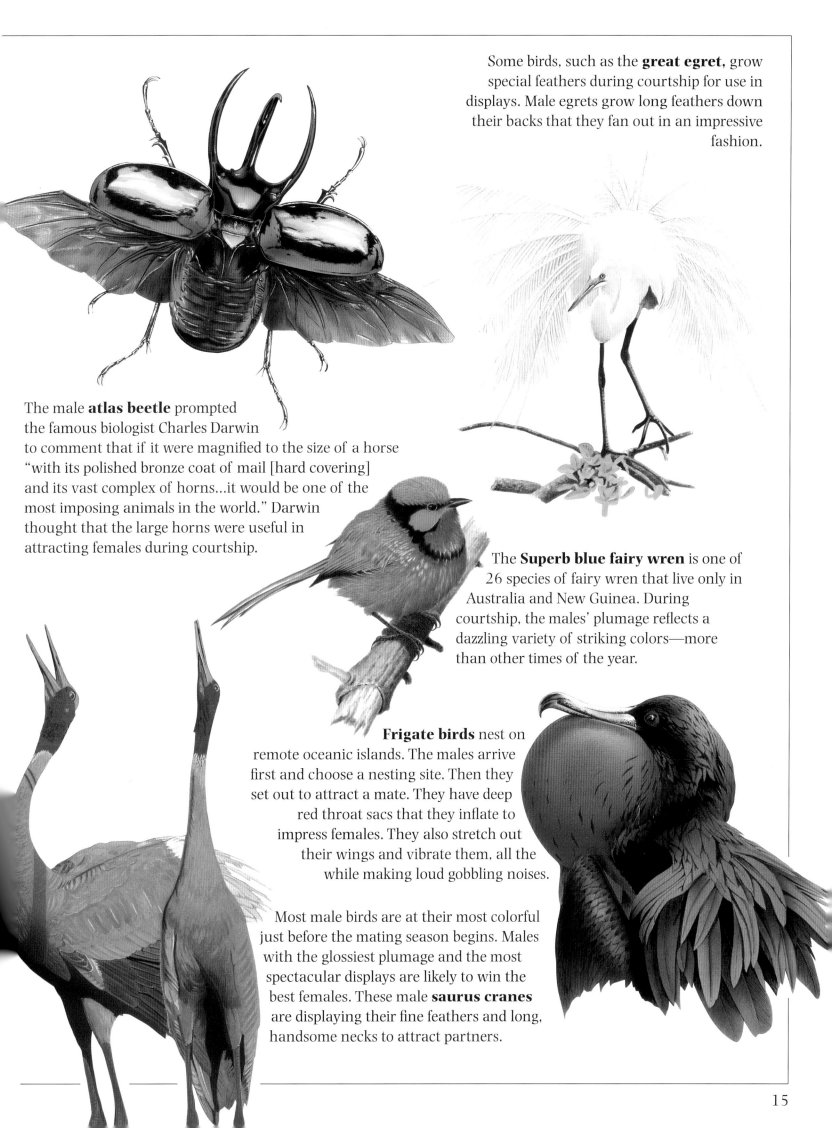

Some birds, such as the **great egret**, grow special feathers during courtship for use in displays. Male egrets grow long feathers down their backs that they fan out in an impressive fashion.

The male **atlas beetle** prompted the famous biologist Charles Darwin to comment that if it were magnified to the size of a horse "with its polished bronze coat of mail [hard covering] and its vast complex of horns...it would be one of the most imposing animals in the world." Darwin thought that the large horns were useful in attracting females during courtship.

The **Superb blue fairy wren** is one of 26 species of fairy wren that live only in Australia and New Guinea. During courtship, the males' plumage reflects a dazzling variety of striking colors—more than other times of the year.

Frigate birds nest on remote oceanic islands. The males arrive first and choose a nesting site. Then they set out to attract a mate. They have deep red throat sacs that they inflate to impress females. They also stretch out their wings and vibrate them, all the while making loud gobbling noises.

Most male birds are at their most colorful just before the mating season begins. Males with the glossiest plumage and the most spectacular displays are likely to win the best females. These male **saurus cranes** are displaying their fine feathers and long, handsome necks to attract partners.

Choosing a Partner

CHECK ME OUT! In spring, male sage grouse form special groups, called leks, on established lekking grounds or arenas. The birds gather together in a strict hierarchy, with the most dominant male at the center. Then the display begins. With pointed tail feathers splayed out, and huge air sacs inflated beneath their white neck feathers, the males create their stunning white ruffs. They also make deep-voiced calls and deflate their neck sacs quickly to make a loud whipping noise. As the females pass among the group, they choose the male that impresses them most.

Male **swallows** have longer feathers on their forked tails than the females. Biologists have noticed that female swallows prefer males with the longest tails. Because the healthiest birds grow the longest tails, they are the most fit and most likely to mate. Sometimes they mate early enough to produce two broods in one summer.

Wolves live in highly organized packs as large as 20 to 30 individuals. Usually only one male and one female from a pack will mate each year. The dominant male and female, known as the alpha pair, bond for one or more breeding seasons. Fighting is common among both males and females as they struggle to become dominant.

Choosing a Partner

Choosing the "right" partner is at at the very heart of courtship. Without an acceptable mate, reproduction becomes compromised. The instinct to reproduce and the need to find a strong, healthy mate who is able to pass along traits that contribute to the species' survival are the two factors that drive the courtship process. Males and females provide signals that make mate choice easier. In addition to visual cues, many animals use odors or physical contact to stimulate action on both sides.

Hares have an excellent sense of smell that is useful during courtship. When the female hare is ready to mate, her body releases a special odor. Male hares are especially sensitive to this smell. This illustration shows several male hares chasing after a female that is "in heat" (ready to mate).

Some animals mate for life. **Masked lovebirds** are small, brightly colored African parrots. They are called "lovebirds" because of the special bond that forms between a male and female pair. They nearly always sit very close to each other and frequently rub beaks and groom each other.

Some female **deep-sea angler fish** grow up to 15 times larger than the males. The male fish have pincer-like teeth. During the breeding season, they bite into the female's skin to hold on to her while they fertilize her eggs. The male stays attached to the female for the rest of their lives, and he is totally dependent on her for food and protection.

During courtship, the male **bald eagle** calls the female with loud, piercing cries. If the female replies, the pair grips talons in midair and performs a tumbling, cartwheeling dance across the sky before mating.

Some animals, like this male **bighorn sheep**, have an odor-sensitive organ in the top of their mouths that they use to pick up odors released by females. The male lifts his head and bares his teeth in what is known as the "flehmen response." By doing this, he can tell whether the female is ready to mate.

Male **sea lions** are much larger than the females. Despite her size, if the female is not "in heat," she will reject the big bull's advances.

These **black-tailed prairie dogs** "kiss" during courtship. In a highly organized prairie dog group, called a coterie, there is usually one male for every four females.

Offerings

PROVING ONESELF. Like many birds, male and female Arctic terns share the job of raising their young. That is why it is important for the females to be sure a potential mate can provide food for their young. To prove that they will be good fathers and providers, the males catch fish and hold them in their beaks until a female accepts them. She then waits to see how many more fish he will bring before she makes her final choice. Eating lots of fish before the breeding season is also good for the female. It helps her build up reserves of fat so she can lay more—and bigger—eggs.

Male **balloon flies** produce silken thread that they weave into large, empty balloons. They apparently use these gifts to impress potential mates. Even though the balloon has no food value, the female accepts it before allowing the male to mate with her.

Offerings

With some animals, a male will have a much better chance of mating if he offers his partner a gift. Most courting gifts consist of items the female can eat. Not only does a gift of food make an impression on the female, it also gives her extra nutrition at a time she most needs it—in preparation for laying eggs or giving birth. Sometimes a gift of food is offered by a male as a distraction. While the female is feeding, he will take advantage and mate with her. Gifts can also be used by the male to prove his ability as a hunter. This indicates to his partner that his offspring will be good hunters.

The **oribi** is a dwarf antelope that lives in many parts of southern and central Africa. During courtship, the male covers the female with a special scented secretion produced in glands beneath his ears.

The male **katydid** gives his gift during mating by transferring a package of high-protein food to the female together with his sperm. The female feasts on the food parcel he leaves her.

Most male **hanging flies** give their partners an insect as a courtship gift. The larger the insect gift, the longer he will be allowed to mate as the female eats it.

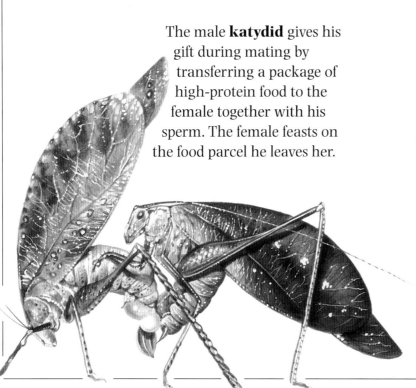

Western grebes perform a rushing ceremony as well as another ritual that involves the presentation of weeds. During courtship, both birds dive for weeds. Then they swim toward each other until their beaks are almost touching. They lift their bodies up and rock their heads with the weeds dangling from their beaks.

Some of the most complex courtship rituals occur among different species of grebes. In some cases, the birds form a lifelong bond. Their springtime premating rituals often consist of getting to know each other again after their winter separation. These **western grebes** are performing a special "rushing" ceremony where both birds rise up out of the water and rush along for about 100 feet (30 m).

The male **nursery web spider** is the only species of spider in the world that gives a courtship gift. He holds his silk-wrapped offering up so that the female can see it. If she is not interested, she will either scuttle away or attack him.

Male **roadrunners** court females by using a variety of techniques, including tail wags, special calls, and gifts of food. The male spends a good deal of time and effort catching lizards and other tasty treats, which proves his stamina and strength.

During the mating season, female **dance flies** are presented with gifts throughout the day. The females feast on the gifts as the males mate with them. The females then fly on to another male who offers a gift as they mate with him. This enables the females to feed very well for 2 to 3 weeks and ensures that one of the strong males is the father.

Fighting It Out

DESIRE FOR DOMINANCE. Male kangaroos fight for the right to mate with one or more females. Before they begin fighting, they perform a stiff-legged walk as they face each other. This is followed by scratching and grooming. When the grooming is done, the males launch into each other. First the forearms are locked together. Then they begin to kick each other with their hind legs. The winner becomes the dominant male in the group, commonly referred to in Australia as the "old man" or "boomer."

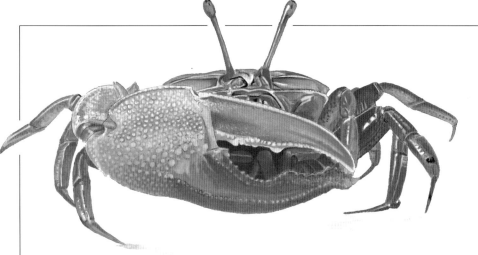

Male **fiddler crabs** have one very large front claw that they move backwards and forwards as though they were playing a violin (hence their name). The claw is used mostly to fight against other males at mating time.

Usually it is the males that fight for mating rights, but female **jackdaws** who do not have mates will court an unattached male. If more than one female is interested in the same male, fights between females can occur.

Fighting It Out

As the mating season approaches, many males fight each other for the right to mate with the females. In some species, the males fight to establish harems (groups of females to which only the dominant male has the access to mate). Among others, individuals fight it out for the rights to unattached females. Sometimes the fighting is fierce with a risk of getting hurt. Other animals use menacing noises or displays to establish dominance without actually coming to blows.

Komodo dragons live on a few islands in Indonesia. Some adults grow up to 10 feet (3 m) in length, making them the largest lizards in the world. At the beginning of the mating season, the males engage in vigorous battles to gain control of a mating territory.

Male **stag beetles** have much larger mandibles (jaws) than the females. They use them to fight at courtship time.

In spring, male **elephant seals** stake out a piece of territory on shore and try to establish a harem of females. Since many males arrive at the same time, fierce fighting ensues. The battles continue until one champion bull remains. Only then do the females come ashore.

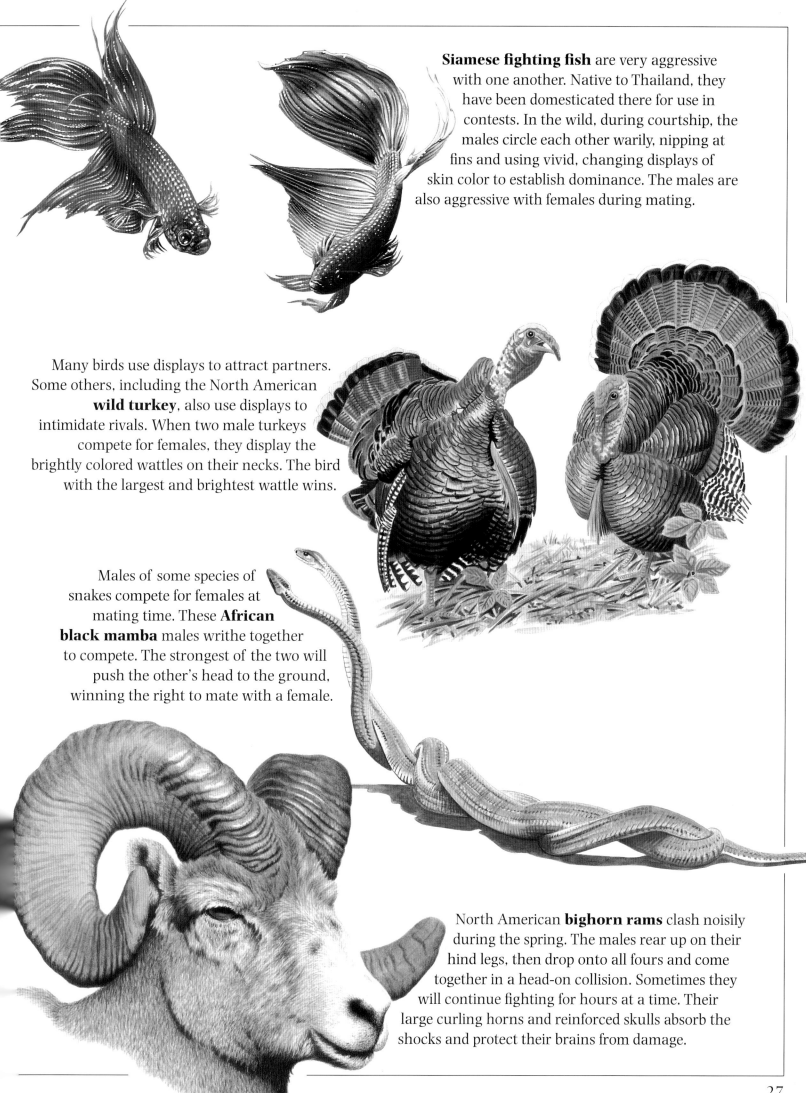

Siamese fighting fish are very aggressive with one another. Native to Thailand, they have been domesticated there for use in contests. In the wild, during courtship, the males circle each other warily, nipping at fins and using vivid, changing displays of skin color to establish dominance. The males are also aggressive with females during mating.

Many birds use displays to attract partners. Some others, including the North American **wild turkey**, also use displays to intimidate rivals. When two male turkeys compete for females, they display the brightly colored wattles on their necks. The bird with the largest and brightest wattle wins.

Males of some species of snakes compete for females at mating time. These **African black mamba** males writhe together to compete. The strongest of the two will push the other's head to the ground, winning the right to mate with a female.

North American **bighorn rams** clash noisily during the spring. The males rear up on their hind legs, then drop onto all fours and come together in a head-on collision. Sometimes they will continue fighting for hours at a time. Their large curling horns and reinforced skulls absorb the shocks and protect their brains from damage.

27

Nests and Dens

STAY-AT-HOME DADS. In spring, the male penduline titmouse prepares a nest using long, tough strands of plant or animal material. When he has almost finished, he sits inside and sings to attract a partner. Females come to inspect the nest. If one likes it, she will help him to finish the nest by lining the inside with soft fibers, such as wool. She then lays five or six eggs, which hatch in two to three weeks. Both parents care for the young.

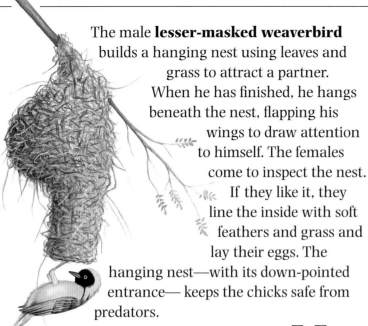

The male **lesser-masked weaverbird** builds a hanging nest using leaves and grass to attract a partner. When he has finished, he hangs beneath the nest, flapping his wings to draw attention to himself. The females come to inspect the nest. If they like it, they line the inside with soft feathers and grass and lay their eggs. The hanging nest—with its down-pointed entrance— keeps the chicks safe from predators.

Dung-rolling scarab beetles cut and shape animal excrement into balls that they bury. These dung balls act as brooding chambers for eggs and as a source of food for larvae when they hatch. The adult pair only mates after they have prepared a dung ball brooding chamber for their eggs.

Nests and Dens

Many animals build a nest or den in which to lay their eggs and bring up their young. The choice of the nesting site, or the construction of the nest, often plays an important role in courtship. Sometimes the males will compete to attract females by trying to build the most spectacular nest. Among bowerbirds in northern Australia and New Guinea, food is easy to come by and feeding requires only a few minutes each day. This allows males to spend almost all their lives building elaborate bowers with the sole purpose of trying to impress a mate.

1

2

During courtship the male southern European **rodeo fish** leads the female toward a mussel (1). When they get to the mussel, the female inserts her ovipositor (egg-placer) into the opening in the mussel shell and lays her eggs (2). The male fish then releases his sperm above the opening so that the eggs are fertilized.

Male **bowerbirds** spend nearly all their time constructing bowers to impress a mate. The bowers are not nests and are only used to attract a partner. Some of the bowers are quite elaborate and are beautifully decorated with colorful fruit, feathers, flowers, and any other useful object the male can find. This large bower (right) was built by the **Vogelkop gardener bowerbird** in New Guinea.

The male **white stork** selects a nesting site and builds a nest. He then sets out to attract a female with a series of displays and calls. When a female accepts, they mate. They both work to bring up their young. White storks often build their nests close to farmhouses because they know a farm will offer a constant source of food.

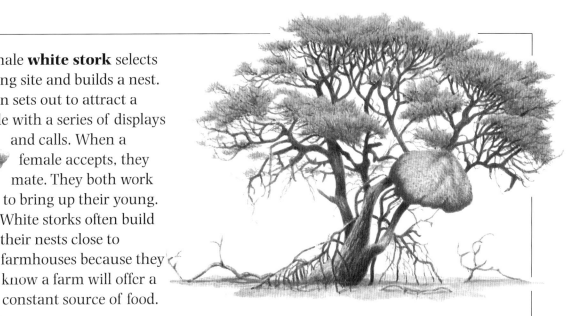

Male **social weaverbirds** work together to build gigantic collective nests with places for over 100 pairs. Once the main structure is in place, each male completes his own opening and egg-laying space for his mate.

Fulmar petrels nest on rocky cliffs without even building a nest. The male and female usually pair for several years, meeting each spring at the same nesting site. The birds only leave each other if they cannot breed.

Male **redstarts** return from their wintering areas in Africa a day or two ahead of the females so that they will have time to choose a nesting area before the females arrive. When the females appear, the males show off the places they have found until a female chooses one. The female then builds the nest.

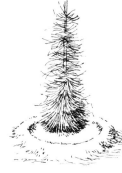
Satin gardener bower.

MacGregor's gardener bower.

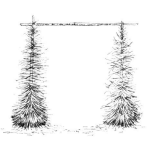
Golden gardener bower.

Striped gardener bower.

Dangers

COURTING DISASTER. Male tungara frogs use loud nocturnal calls to attract a mate. Unfortunately for them, their serenades can also attract predators. Bats recognize the tungara's calls and will follow them to find their prey. To protect themselves, the frogs often form large groups while singing so there is less chance of being eaten. If they are alone, they may modify their song, using a low whining noise rather than the usual series of whines and clicks.

Courtship and mating among the larger species of cats, including **lions**, can involve aggression between the males and females. Contact during courtship can reduce aggression levels, although it sometimes continues through mating.

Dangers

There are many dangers involved in courtship and breeding. The fierce competition between males for the right to mate with females can lead to injury. As happens with the tungara frog, advertising one's presence with loud calls or displays can also attract predators. In some species of insects, including the praying mantis shown here, there is even a danger of being eaten by one's partner after mating. And the dangers of reproducing don't end with successful mating; protecting eggs and hatchlings also involves many hazards!

Male **musk deer** have two large teeth in their upper jaws. Measuring up to 2.75 inches (7 cm) in length, these sharp teeth can inflict painful wounds during battles with other males. Sometimes the wounds are fatal.

Male **praying mantises** are drawn to females by their scent. The much larger females are normally willing to mate but they are also quite aggressive. Males must approach them with caution. After they have mated, the male has to escape quickly or risk being eaten. The females attempt to eat their partners in order to get nutrients for their eggs.

Among **spiders**, the female is often much larger than the male. At mating time, the male has to be very careful when approaching the female. If she mistakes him for prey, she will eat him. Female spiders of some species devour their partners after mating.

Some birds, including the **Senagalese sand grouse**, build no nests and prefer to lay their eggs in dips or hollows in the ground. This leaves both the eggs and the parents more vulnerable to attack during incubation.

Some attempt has been made to keep these **sand grouse** eggs safe by pushing stones into a perimeter around the nest. From above, the eggs will actually be quite difficult to see because their sandy color camouflages them well in the beige desert sands.

In many animal species the females mate with several males. Some prospective fathers have developed ways of ensuring that their sperm fertilizes the female's eggs. The male **damsel fly** has a special barbed penis with which he removes the sperm of competing males while mating.

The possible hazards of reproduction continue after successful courtship and mating. After the male **midwife frog** has fertilized his partner's eggs, he winds the sticky string of eggs around his waist and hind legs. He carries the eggs around with him, keeping them safe from predators until they hatch about one month later.

Mating

When courtship is successful, it leads to mating. To ensure survival, male and female animals must make sure that their sex cells (egg and sperm) come into contact with each other. When this happens, fertilization occurs, and a new individual is created. Mating can take place in many different ways. Internal fertilization is common among most land animals, including insects. Among aquatic animals, fertilization usually occurs externally, once the eggs are outside the mother's body.

At mating time male and female **scorpions** clutch each other by the pincers and begin a stately dance. The male drops a package of sperm onto the ground and gradually pulls the female over the top of it. The sperm package attaches itself to her, and soon her eggs are fertilized.

Grasshopper males sing to attract a mate by rubbing their wings and legs together to produce a loud chirping noise. When a female comes along, the male climbs onto her back, grips her sides, and fertilizes her eggs internally. The female then uses her ovipositor (egg-placer) to deposit the eggs in the ground, where they will stay safe until they hatch.

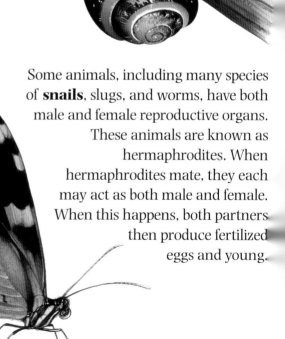

Some animals, including many species of **snails**, slugs, and worms, have both male and female reproductive organs. These animals are known as hermaphrodites. When hermaphrodites mate, they each may act as both male and female. When this happens, both partners then produce fertilized eggs and young.

Among **butterflies**, courtship usually consists of a series of movements, in a kind of ritualized dance. Each species has a slightly different courtship dance. At the end of the dance, the male transfers his sperm to the female, which fertilizes her eggs.

When female **garter snakes** emerge from their winter hibernation pits in the rocks, they emit a special scent that tells the male snakes it is mating time. Each female is immediately surrounded by dozens of males who attempt to mate with her. When one of the males is successful, she switches off her scent signal and they all depart.

Corals live in warm tropical seas. The tiny soft-bodied polyps secrete a hard substance from which coral reefs are formed. They mate on just a few nights each year. When the sea reaches just the right temperature, the animals release packages of thousands of sperm and eggs. Because the eggs and sperm are released at the same time, they mingle, and external fertilization occurs in the water.

Dolphins are social animals that usually engage in long courtship rituals. Mating itself is quite brief. The pair only stays belly to belly for a matter of minutes.

Among **sea urchins**, the female releases her eggs into the sea and the male releases sperm, which fertilizes them. After fertilization, each egg begins to divide and multiply into additional cells. The illustrations below show the egg: 1) before fertilization; 2) after the first division into two cells; 3) after the second division into four cells; 4) after the third division into eight cells; 5) and several divisions later as the animal develops into a multi-celled embryo.

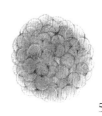

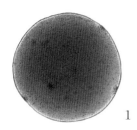  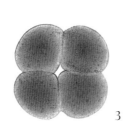 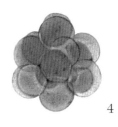

1   2   3   4   5

For More Information

Books

Amos, Janine. *Animals* (Picture Reference). Chicago, IL: World Book Inc., 1997.

Kerrod, Robin. *Facts on File Wildlife Atlas*. New York, NY: Checkmark Books, 1998.

Parker, Steve. *Eyewitness: Mammal* (Dorling Kindersley Eyewitness Books). New York, NY: Dorling Kindersley, 2000.

Walters, Martin. *Wildlife* (Factfinder Series). New York, NY: Smithmark Publishing, 1999.

Web Site

National Wildlife Federation

www.nwf.org/kids

Learn wildlife facts and visit animal homes.

Index

Africa, 14, 22

African black mamba, 27

Alpha pair, 18

Angler fish, 19

Arctic terns, 20–21

Asia, 10

Atlas beetle, 15

Australia, 15, 24, 30

Bald eagle, 19

Balloon flies, 22

Bats, 32

Beetles, 30

Bighorn rams, 27

Bighorn sheep, 19

Boobies, 14

Bowerbirds, 30

Butterflies, 36

Cobs, 10

Corals, 37

Coterie, 19

Cygnets, 10

Damsel fly, 35

Dance flies, 23

Darwin, Charles, 15

Dolphins, 37

Egret, 15

Elephant seals, 26

Elk, 11

Embryo, 37

Europe, 10

Fairy wren, 15

Fiddler crabs, 26

Frigate birds, 15

Frogs, 11, 32–35

Fulmar petrels, 31

Garter snakes, 37

Grasshopper, 36

Great argus pheasant, 14

Great reed warblers, 10

Grebes, 23

Hanging flies, 22

Hares, 10, 18

Hermaphrodites, 36

Hoverflies, 10

Humpback whales, 8, 11

Jackdaws, 26

Kangaroos, 24–25

Katydid, 22

Komodo dragons, 26

Leks, 16

Lesser-masked weaverbird, 30

Lions, 34

Lizards, 23, 26

Mandrills, 14

Marmots, 11

Masked lovebirds, 18

Midwife frog, 35

Musk deer, 34

Mussel, 30

New Guinea, 15, 30

North America, 10

Nursery web spider, 23

Nyala antelope, 14

Oribi, 22

Parrots, 18

Peacock, 12–13

Penduline titmouse, 28

Pens, 10

Pikas, 10

Polyps, 37

Prairie dogs, 19

Praying mantises, 34

Rabbits, 10

Redstarts, 31

Roadrunners, 23

Rodeo fish, 30

Sable antelope, 10–11

Sage grouse, 16–17

Saurus cranes, 15

Scorpions, 36

Sea lions, 19

Sea urchins, 37

Senagalese sand grouse, 35

Siamese fighting fish, 27

Slugs, 36

Social weaverbirds, 31

South America, 14

Snails, 36

Spiders, 34

Stag beetles, 26

Stags, 11

Swallows, 18

Thailand, 27

White stork, 31

Whooper swans, 10

Wild turkey, 27

Wolves, 18

Worms, 36